THE LIFE OF ST. DESIDERIUS

Sisebut,
King of Visigoths

Translated by: D.P. Curtin

Dalcassian Publishing Company
PHILADELPHIA, PA

THE LIFE OF ST. DESIDERIUS

Copyright @ 2014 Dalcassian Publishing Company

All rights reserved. No part of this publication may be reproduced, distributed, or transmitted in any form or by any means, including photocopying, recording, or other electronic or mechanical methods, without the prior written permission of the publisher, except in the case of brief quotations embodied in critical reviews and certain other non-commercial uses permitted by copyright law. For permission request, write to Dalcassian Publishing Company at dalcassianpublishing at gmail.com

ISBN: 979-8-8691-7508-3 (Paperback)

Library of Congress Control Number:
Author: Curtin, D.P. (1985-)

Printed by Ingram Content Group, 1 Ingram Blvd, La Vergne, Tennessee

First printing edition 2014.

The Life of St. Desiderius

1. For the sake of the record of history, for the edification of men to come, for the holy pursuits of the succeeding times, I arranged to write the life of the holy martyr, Desiderius, who was known to us by the fame of his faithfulness. That is to say, this was to be done more by the pen than by spoken words burdened by falsehood, which begged us to be present to the coming of the Lord, who by his acts of virtues, did not give him undeserved ability to act.

2. This man was born of illustrious Roman parents, consecrated to God from his very cradle, and had quite a noble lineage. When he had reached the age at which it was lawful to be taught, he was given over to the study of literature. He was not much more than an infant, but with increasing vigor, already learned and contemplative, he was fully taught in grammar. He, thereafter, spoke of the divine authorities with surprising speed. According to the proscriptions of the Gospel, he offered food to the hungry, drink to the thirsty, he provided comfort to the sick and imprisoned, shelter to the stranger, and clothed the naked with his garments. He was not praised by all of his enemy's exaltation of virtues, as he was not saved by languid drunkenness. He was not enraptured by the excessive presumption of food and not corrupted by a voracious lust. He was not deceived by lying and was not persuaded by greed to

harm others. Nor was he taken by such divine favor that he was polluting his own virtues when the motions of puberty had not yet ended. He did not seize his youthful years. He did not seize his own desires, or the fame of growing a good opinion of himself. He spread the works of light, pardoned by the true light, which shone in many nations for the benefits of various cities. When the people took hold of him, the bishops themselves demanded the saint, who with the reluctance of the great mystery of humility, confessed himself on the tree.

3. In the end it was not so voluntary, the impulse felt by many prayers that the priests of Vienne made, which he received, by careful preaching he removed the quarrelsome from anger, the deceit from the deceitful, the covetous from rapacity, the lustful from succumbing to iniquities. He tamed drunkenness with sobriety, overcame gluttony with abstinence, overcame discord with the office of charity, checked pride with sincere humility, shook the uncertainty from torpor by vigilance, taught them to be generous in almsgiving. But he taught all these things by example rather than by words, knowing that the Lord would come, and not so much by words as by works.

4. While these things were being carried on by yielding to Christ, the allocator and friend of death groaned against the converted, and against the soldier of Christ he brought on himself a hedge of weapons of every kind, ready to fight. Of course, the cunning of the adversary did not prevail, nothing taught the power of his calamitous wickedness, whom the grace of the Redeemer armed with special weapons. At length the wicked Spirit smote a certain man of malignant mind with a viperous disease, and poured into his bowels the poisoned cup of the contemplation of many crimes, to the extent that he increased his evil mouth with evil senses, slandered the athlete of the Lord with his thoughts, and persuaded some to compare in his name against the servant of the Savior. The swindler forged such documents of fraud. They meet together with a certain matron, who was of noble lineage, ugly in mind, but just in name. Ugly in deed, but honorable in title, but more dishonorable in deed and unworthy of good. She was evidently laden with evil, never discreet from external truth, or from criminality. In the council, it was asked of the most blessed that Desiderius be subjected to violence. Therefore, the senators sent a

verdict against the innocent one, having long ago adapted their machinations, and gave a blessing to the reckless venture. The people immediately punished him, deprived him of honor, and bound him in exile to a monastery on the island. The rejection of which was the greatest happiness, the insult visible sanctity, his degradation was a sign of eternal happiness. A false priest was substituted for him, indeed by name Domnulus, truly a servant of the devil, and as much as the man of God grew in abundant virtues, on the contrary, he was disgusting with evil deeds.

5. Indeed, in that monastery, when the blessed martyr was living a consecrated life, there came a poor man begging for kindling, whose lips were closed by innate silence, and the duty of his articulate voice was obscured by perpetual silence. Whom the Almighty Father, not ignoring the prayer of his soldiers, made him ready and fit for office and speech. Namely, that which had been done by the opinion of the crows, the good report could not keep silent, but rather, surveying everything, brought what transpired to the knowledge of many. Whence it came to pass that multitudes of the languishing ran to him in the hope of recovering their salvation, and there was no lack of the Lord's favors for healing, for which the servant of God implored the Lord. Sufficiently, as I think, has flashed the general discourse of healing by grace; but in order not to close the door of scrutiny by observing that tidy speech is often too brief, I have especially endeavored to show that, wherever I could, I made some continuation of this work. Some of the ancients, who are always shrouded in darkness, occupied the time of night, and their faces had no light cast upon them, whom the Sunday soldier, sequestered by the hideous veil of darkness, recalled to their heads a bright light by the grace of God. Where three lepers were cured by St. Desiderius.

6. After these things, three lepers, oppressed by their disease, came to him for the grace of healing, whose bodies had been invaded by an ugly white mass, and whose wounds were besieged with the unfortunate frame of dark marks. The stench was intolerable, and the vertiginous quality of the face was exceedingly and abundantly horrible. The foul humor eviscerated almost the entire stomach, and the purulent contagion, cut off the hair, drew shamefully by the

THE LIFE OF ST. DESIDERIUS

roots. The servant of God removed the morbid passions of those who labored, and restored healthy and cheerful ones to their own salvation. With her usual excellent piety to the Lord, he planted in the ears of Theoderic the rumor of the people and of Brunigild as well, that the servant of God, who was exalted by his rich virtues, and that the gift of healing was imparted to him by the gift of omnipotent power. At once, alarmed and struck with the greatest fear, they scrutinize the detailed facts of the matter, insofar as either the honor due would be rendered to the banished, or the permanence of banishment would be added to the condemned in vain. When an investigation laboriously discovered the cause of the whole mystery, the inventor of the magical art of the nefarious plan, who had long ago been seen to have condemned the soldier of Christ, was rebuked by divine vengeance, not undeservedly worthy, of the detestable outcome I noted with a continuous narrative. This pestilential person, and unhappily remembered, was held liable to many vices and crimes. Yet, among his nefarious crimes was the covetousness of riches, and crimination, which aroused the greatest of the people to kill the monstrous disgrace. For at a certain time, while he was standing by the looks of his supporter, Theuderic, he was deceived by a tumultuous destruction at the hands of the Burgundians. In vain, the corpse was left slain and bleeding here and there. In this way he lost his life and his soul at the same time, a wretched being, and with the infernal barriers he mingled himself to destruction. What about that unjustly justice and those who are justly unjust? Whom he so bloodily seized as truly his own property? At the same time as the one already mentioned was slain, an evil spirit invaded it. And all the forces of falsity which he had not long since fitted, from home again he spent too much in the same fatal spring, whose exacting profession was brought forth in this manner. "I know the crime of God devised against the servant. I know the cause. I know more feelingly and the due punishment. May this Almighty avenger respond to Brunigild's plan, the avenger restore these punishments, and the right hand of Him inflict sufferings on the avenger, whose persuasion drew me to destruction with smoke, an oath to death, a promise to no perishment, but salvation." When he had made an end of speaking, the master of vices, enraged and suffocated, perished. Hearing of the deaths of the aforementioned Brunigildis and Theodoric at the same time, he was frightened.

THE LIFE OF ST. DESIDERIUS

7. Thinking that such things would be done by the divine judgment, they feared more venomously, and lest the witnesses should be fined by the sentence of observation, they ordered with disguised piety that the man of God, who had been removed from the priestly order in vain, should come again to govern his own church. As long as he nodded less to their demands, and he affirmed that he would remain where he had been exiled, and again offered prayers. He asked them not to deny his presence to them, and to loosen the restraints of their frauds with a clement mind. Indeed, sincere piety warmed the sincere breast, and abundant benevolence opened the way for the servant of God to regress. But when the face of the unfortunate man revealed himself to be the Blessed One, his supporters fell at his feet, and they strove to propitiate him whom they had so recently relegated by fraudulent condemnation, and that the atonement of such a small, pious man would free them from the harm that the strangers whom the fatal contagion had made implicit in the crimes. He relaxed the deed he had committed with a merciful heart, and according to the sentence of the Lord he did not withhold the guilt of those who owed it, but omitted it. At length, with the greatest supply, he was unhappily struck down, and the Church of Vienna received its exultant governor. They rejoiced that the sick man had found a physician, that he had found comfort for the oppressed, and that the needy had already received food. What a lot is this? Copious votes were given by the Lord of the Viennese Church; for the presence of the holy man, in pity for the Lord, suspends the calamities, shortages, and the frequent ravages of the pestilence, and the unusual storms of the whole city, which, without doubt, the removal of the pastor, by reason of his absence, had oppressed.

8. Of his virtues, I set out to narrate three things about his virtues, when he labored with a languid speech from any disease of inactivity. While at a certain time a large crowd had gathered to visit him, he commanded them to refresh themselves with food and drink as usual, and it was told by the minister that he had failed in the more and more desired kind of wine. Quickly that vessel into which such liquid had already flowed, he commanded himself to be shown. That which had been prefigured by the protection of the cross, was filled with the mere fragrance of the grace of the Savior. Thus the appropriate crowd was

refreshed at the same time with a benediction and a mystical drink. Again, after a long distraction, he was soaking his body in abstinence, and chastising himself with the perception of the flesh, not for impurity, but for temperance. In the intervening time, his priest came not far from the city to visit him. It is here that Phoebus, in passing through the spaces of the day, had crossed the axis of the hours, and the legitimate time of restoration was imminent. With a sudden change in the air, with feathers rustling and flying swiftly, an eagle, the queen of birds, appeared from the shining parts of the sky, who, carrying a watery stew, set forth a fair amount of cattle before their faces, which, being received with the greatest delight by the generous Lord, they bowed joyfully before some of their noble retinue. At the time of the passion, he filled the lamp with his own hands and lit it near the altar, which radiated less elongated shafts of light, and the measure of its capacity was increased without any objection [...] The liquid, of course, was overflowing with oil. He was embraced by the highest reason who, by the grace of God, pellets the infirmities of labor, and removes morbid human sufferings by conferring salvation. Of course, it is sufficient to have said about his life that I was able to briefly summarize it in exhaustive speech. Now concerning his sufferings, how he consigned his holy soul to the Almighty Lord, that they may be brought to our notice, by his own support, to be expedient.

9. When it would not be useful, but rather obstinate, rather to destroy than to rule, Theuderic and Brunegild were both seen to be hostile to all vices. The curse of perjury was unlocked and the covenants of the sacrament were deserted by the mind of sacrilegious treachery, so as not to attempt to be unfaithful. None of the crimes or deeds remained at that time. God's martyr, the inspector and priest of these evils, appeared in prophetic fashion, with a blare of the trumpet. The vessels of wrath and foment of vices, and the bush of damnation bitter for the sweet, harsh for the mild, he offered deadly medicines for salvation, and a more savage enemy besieged their breast. The most cunning serpent held captives in his dominion. Nor could they reach the harbor of safety with free steps, to whom the fatal robber had attached tighter bonds. Satisfied, however, with his light cups, they began to bark rabid words against the servant of God, and to vomit the foulest voices threatening them with noisy

THE LIFE OF ST. DESIDERIUS

words. Yet, the martyr of God was not broken by the threat of mortals, nor softened by the wrath of the perfidious, nor bent by the tempest of the insane. He offered himself unmoved to be smitten by justice in the persecutions, had he not taken the promised ethereal kingdom from the Lord. This enemy, beholding the steadfastness of humanity, who had never forsaken the bosoms of Brunigild and Theuderic, mingled himself entirely as in his own home, and in an imperative manner, thrust his efforts to more destruction. Promising to give them the first place in punishments, if they could free the soul of Christ's soldier from his bodily bonds to extract. At once the sacrilegious mouth opened with noxious words, and always armed with abuses, offered a sentence of impiety. Desire, hostile to our manners, and enemy to our works, beaten with the blows of a stone, and afflicted with many kinds of punishments, was pleasing to notice. The officers, compared the charge of such a heinous law, promised to carry out the edict of the emperor, whom they most unwillingly took into their ears. Nor did the martyr of God hide the struggles of his labor, for he had been predestined, nay, forewarned by the Lord, to receive the rewards of the crown. When he saw the day approaching, he was suddenly snatched from the bosom of the church by the hands of the unfaithful, and led to execution as if he were a guilty man who was about to be killed. "Why do you leave the flock to perish? Do not, we beseech you, send us into the mouths of the wolves, lest your sheep, until now sweetly fed with nectarine flowers, be driven away by the biting thorn and briers of a less procuring priest. It is indeed certain, and the word is in harmony with the divine letter, that the absence of the shepherd is the scattering of the sheep, whose presence is of the greatest benefit. On no account do we allow you to be taken away from us, who are equally denied the life they desire, may he suffer a glorious death with you". Finally, with these calm words, the blessed martyr brought forth his words: "an admirable intention indeed, but not a praiseworthy devotion. If the Tartars were to besiege us at the gates of the cave, if the gates of hell were trying to shut up the funeral pyres, if the horrendous flame of the barbarians were trying to invade with a crackling sound, I would have agreed to attack the enemy more fiercely with spiritual weapons; now, since the ethereals are invited into the military camp with the radiant angelic hosts, with the apostles and apostolic men, with the shining groups of martyrs, the universe is returned to us and yours. I request you to allow your shepherd to return to the shepherd of all shepherds, so that the flock may arrive more easily, before the priest, unblemished and ready for the place." Thus he said, "and behold, suddenly a packed group of madmen came furiously, men of fatal and terrible countenance, whose brows were grim, their eyes cruel, their looks hateful, their movements horrible. And they were sinister in mind, perverse in character, liars in tongue, obscene in speech, outwardly turgid, inwardly empty, ugly in both ways, unworthy of good things, rich of the worst, prone to crimes, enemies of God, friends of the devil indeed, perpetually vindictive to the point of death." Ministering the cursed destruction of these with fury, he snatched away the weapons of the most wicked, and poured a shower of stony heart upon the martyr of Christ; which, when the ferocious darts of the madmen passed over Marseilles, and turned their course in another direction, the flint being the hardest by nature, and the very crash of the stoning of God presented itself to the servants of God, and every non-living thing was cut down by God's laws, yet living by the divine laws, the human breast remained only hardened, because it was prone in it might be out of pity, and driven away. When he had breathed his last, he seized the same and broke the neck of the blessed man with a club. Thus, the soul abandoned the body, and stripped herself of the bonds of the flesh, so that the conqueror mingled his ears with the count of the astrigers.

10. Life and death at the same time, unpolished as he could, he told the words of Christ's soldiers, who displeases all the cruelty of the authorities, who are too ignorant, abandoning the pomp of words, and he ennobled those lowly and who believe. Therefore, as we have described his life, his virtues, and his grandly glorious end, it remains for us to narrate the destruction and death of the lost. When Theuderic, forsaking God, rejecting the Almighty, rejoiced when he heard the message of Christ about the servant, he was seized with dysentery, and he lost a most hideous life, and acquired for himself a perpetual friend. He lost the lost comfort of Brunigild, and he was tormented with a terrible inner conscience, so much so that the quality of guilt he had raised in the crime he had committed, the consequent revenge would feed him more keenly by torturing him. While she was rolling with her dark mind, she declared war against a neighboring nation. But when the time for the contest was clear, and a

band of diviners packs went forth, and indeed terror invaded the part of this woman. From which it came to pass that the sick head followed the numbing of the limbs to the protection of the body. Thus, wandering before the face of the opposition, she was first captured by the enemy, the enemy of Christian rule, and the master of all crimes. Of the destruction of which he will not hesitate to say what we have learned from popular opinion. He is a tortuous animal, with a massive body, and having naturally some bends, although the top of the back is more bulging, and when collected, it occupies a higher position than the rest of the frame, it is sufficiently and abundantly suitable for carrying loads, and is superior to other animals for riding. On the pinnacle of this center, the ancients are lifted up, uncovered in their clothes, and brought down ignominiously before the faces of their enemies. For some time he gives a miracle to those who wait most odiously. From then on he is bound by the wild beasts, and is carried away through rough and rugged places. Thus the body, already soaked in old age, is plucked out in vain by horses, and the dismembered and bloody limbs languish here and there without a name. In this way, the earthly soul of matter is dissolved, and bound by perpetual punishments and not undeservedly, it is held by the burning pitch of the boiling waves. This major prosecution resulted from the occurrence of wider causes. But that he may not displease the fastidious by his prolixity, let us set a limit and an end to those who bind a little in a manner; lamenting the whole community, that they should not too lazily accept that which our Lord Jesus Christ did not hesitate to forgive through his martyrdom, to whose most venerable body Christ will contribute such an abundance of healings. Whenever he was afflicted with any illness, or disturbed by weakness of body, he immediately sought the divine name there with all his heart, dispelling all diseases from himself and driving away the whole stain, and being healthy and cheerful, he reached the desired health by the grace of God; one Lord in the Trinity and ever abiding, who bestows eternal life on the most unworthy follower of me and gives abundant grace to those who hear you.

The Scriptorium Project is the work of a small group of lay people of various apostolic churches who are interested in the preservation, transmission, and translation of the works of the early and medieval church. Our efforts are to make the works of the church fathers accessible to anyone who might have an interest in Christian antiquities and the theological, philosophical, and moral writings that have become the bedrock of Western Civilization.

To-date, our releases have pulled from the Greek, Syriac, Georgian, Latin, Celtic, Ethiopian, and Coptic traditions of Christianity, and have been pulled from sundry local traditions and languages.

Other Titles from the Early Visigothic Church:

Frankish & Visigothic Councils: 549-615 AD (June 2007)
The Life of St. Desiderius by Sisebut, King of Visoths (Oct. 2014)
Chronicle of Marius by Marius Aventicensis (Feb. 2015)
Letters of Sisebut by Sisebut, King of Visigoths (May 2016)
The Eight Vices by Eutropius of Valencia (July 2017)
Visigothic Chronicle by John of Biclaro (Aug. 2018)
Chronicon by Eutrandus of Ticino (Jan. 2019)
The Decree of 610 by Gundemar, King of Visigoths (Mar. 2020)
The Acts of the Martyrs of Caesaraugusta by St. Braulio of Zaragoza (July 2022)

www.ingramcontent.com/pod-product-compliance
Lightning Source LLC
LaVergne TN
LVHW051924060526
838201LV00060B/4167